UNDERSTANDING CHILDREN'S SEXUAL BEHAVIORS

What's Natural And Healthy

TONI CAVANAGH JOHNSON, PH.D.

Institute on Violence, Abuse and Trauma
6160 Cornerstone Court East
San Diego, CA 92121

(858) 623-2777 x 357

Printed in the United States of America
January, 2007

Library of Congress Cataloging-in-Publication Data

Main entry under title:
Understanding Children's Sexual Behaviors – What's Natural And Healthy

This book provides information about children's sexual behaviors.

Written by: Toni Cavanagh Johnson, Ph.D.

Includes bibliographical references
28 pages

ISBN 978-1-882948-19-2

1. Sexual behaviors of children, 2. Parent information, 3. Child development, 4. Child abuse, 5. Sexual abuse, 6. Boundary violations

INTRODUCTION

When a child (under age 12) is engaging in sexual behaviors it is sometimes difficult to decide when the sexual behavior is natural and healthy and when it may be an indication of some distress or disturbance. This booklet provides a definition of natural and healthy childhood sexual behaviors and then contrasts this with 20 characteristics of problematic sexual behaviors in young children. Charts describe children's "natural and healthy" sexual behaviors, behaviors "of concern" and those in need of professional evaluation. Information is provided on how and where to look for help if an evaluation seems warranted. A continuum of childhood sexual behaviors, from natural and healthy to children who sexually offend, is described.

NATURAL AND HEALTHY SEXUAL BEHAVIOR

It is expected that 40-85% of children will engage in at least some sexual behaviors before 13 years of age (Finkelhor, 1983; Friedrich, 1991; Gil & Johnson, 1993; Goldman & Goldman, 1988; Haugaard & Tilly, 1988; Larsson & Svedin, 2001). The following definition will assist in understanding natural and healthy sexual expression in pre-pubertal children. This will be contrasted below with characteristics of childhood sexual expression that are problematic.

Natural and healthy sexual exploration during childhood is an *information gathering process* wherein children *explore* each other's bodies by looking and touching (e.g. playing doctor), as well as explore *gender roles and behaviors* (e.g. playing house). Children involved in natural and healthy sexual play are of *similar age, size and developmental status* and participate on a *voluntary* basis. While siblings engage in *mutual* sexual exploration, most sexual play is between children who have an ongoing mutually enjoyable play and/or school *friendship*. The sexual behaviors are *limited in type and frequency* and occur in *several periods* of the child's life. The child's interest in sex and sexuality is *balanced* by curiosity about other aspects of his or her life. Natural and healthy sexual exploration may result in *embarrassment* but does not usually leave children with deep feelings of anger, shame, fear or anxiety. If the children are discovered in an act of sexual exploration and instructed to stop, the behavior generally *diminishes, at least in the view of adults*. The feelings of the children regarding the sexual behavior are generally *light-hearted and spontaneous*. Generally, children experience pleasurable sensations from genital touching, some children experience sexual arousal, while some children experience orgasm. Sexual arousal and orgasm are more frequently found in older children entering puberty (Johnson & Mitra, 2007).

WHAT CAN AFFECT CHILDREN'S NATURAL AND HEALTHY SEXUAL BEHAVIOR?

Individual differences exist between children across all of their behaviors; sexual behaviors are no different. Children's interest in sex and sexuality can vary from a lot, to a little, or none at all. When thinking back to their childhoods, 72% of a sample of 339 U.S. child welfare and mental health professionals said they engaged in solitary sexual behaviors when they were 12 and younger; 73% recalled engaging in sexual behaviors with other children. In this sample, 48% reported exploring themselves, including genitals, 32% looked at "dirty pictures," 21% masturbated to orgasm, 34% recalled showing their "private parts" to another child, 16% humped or pretended to have intercourse with a child, and 5% put an object (other than their penis) in the vagina or rectum of another child. Sexual stimulation/sexual arousal (as an adult might feel) was recalled by 1.5% of the sample when they were between 2-5 years old, 9% between 6-10 years old, and 25% when they were 11-12 years old (Johnson & Mitra, 2007).

The child's age, the level of stress in the family, family violence, family sexuality and time spent in day-care may also influence the type and frequency of children's sexual behaviors (Friedrich, Fisher, Broughton, Houston, & Shafran, 1998). Children's sexual behaviors, as well as their level of comfort with sexuality, may be affected by the size of the family's living space, the neighborhood in which they live, the age of their siblings, their level of sexual interest, parental, religious, societal and cultural norms and values and attitudes regarding sex and sexuality.

WHAT MIGHT CONTRIBUTE TO A CHILD'S SEXUAL BEHAVIOR MOVING BEYOND WHAT IS CONSIDERED NATURAL AND HEALTHY?

Problematic sexual behaviors may be seen in children who:

- are confused based on what they see on television, videos, video games, magazines, movies, or from "surfing the Net."

- do not receive adequate supervision. When left alone children may be with people who expose them to too much adult or adolescent sexuality.

- live in neighborhoods in which sex is a major influence.

- live in homes with a sexualized environment. Contributing factors can be: parental fights about sex; sexual jealousy of partners; sexual language; sexual jokes; sexual comments about others' bodies; sexual gestures; sexual comments (negative) about men and women; pornography, explicit videos, and R-rated or X-rated movies watched when children are around.

- live in homes where there is little or no physical, sexual or emotional privacy. For instance: bathroom doors have no locks; children are told the details of their parents' sex lives and problems; children's bodies (over age 6) are inspected and discussed, groomed and touched; children must kiss people they don't like, regardless of their discomfort; people do not knock before entering bedrooms or bathrooms; sexual behaviors and nudity occur in living areas of the home regardless of the discomfort of family members.

- have been used to meet a parent's emotional needs which may be sexualized. Almost fulfilling the role of a substitute partner, the child may sleep in the bed with the parent, hear about the parent's problems and/or spend time with the parent shopping and/or going to the movies. The parent overexposes the child to his/her own confused sexual attitudes, behaviors and feelings. This may not constitute overt sexual abuse but covert abuse or emotional incest. It can be highly emotionally, physically and sexually confusing to the child. The child may feel a generalized sexual tension in relation to the parent. The child may be pushed aside when the parent has on adult partner.

- live with parents who act in sexual ways after drinking or taking drugs regardless of the presence of children.
- live in places where sex is routinely paired with aggression, such as fights about sex, violent sexual language or forced sex.
- live in sexually explicit environments in which sex is used in exchange for drugs or to keep from being hurt.
- have been physically and/or emotionally abused and/or neglected.
- have observed physical violence, particularly between their parents/caregivers, due to sexual jealousy and sexual mistrust.
- have been made to observe genitalia or sexual acts for the sexual pleasure of others.
- have been observed or photographed naked for the sexual stimulation of others (children may have been forced to engage in sex acts together).
- have been sexually abused by direct physical contact to their bodies or being used to sexually stimulate others' bodies.
- are physically or hormonally different from other children.

Other factors that are sometimes found in the backgrounds of children with sexual behavior problems are poverty, single parents with little education, many stressful life events, and feelings of rejection by their mothers (Friedrich, Davies, Feher, & Wright, 2003). Additional factors sometimes found are parents with mental or severe physical illness, parents in jail, and the child being placed in foster care (Johnson & Mitra, 2007).

When children's emotional and physical space is routinely violated, it may leave an unconscious feeling of distress related to sex which then manifests itself in increased sexual behaviors. In some children, the level of exposure to adult sexuality is so overwhelming that they are unable to integrate it into their developing sexuality. These children may engage in sexual behaviors to try to diffuse their confusion, tension and anxiety (See pages 22-25).

TWENTY CHARACTERISTICS OF PROBLEMATIC SEXUAL BEHAVIOR IN CHILDREN

The following characteristics can be used to assess whether a child is engaging in sexual behaviors that may require a professional evaluation. If a child's sexual behavior can be described by several of the following characteristics and the child's caretakers cannot find a reasonable and healthy explanation for this, the child should be evaluated by a qualified professional who is knowledgeable about child sexuality or child abuse. A child-sensitive interview regarding possible confusion about sex and sexuality is indicated, bearing in mind that there are many reasons for problematic sexual behaviors (See pages 3-5).

1. The children engaged in the sexual behaviors do not have an ongoing mutual play relationship. Sexual play between children is an extension of regular play behavior. Just as children prefer to play with children with whom they get along, the same is true with sexual play. As most children are very aware of taboos on sexual play in the open, they pick friends who will keep a secret.

2. Sexual behaviors are engaged in by children of different ages or developmental levels. Unless there are no similar-age children in the neighborhood, most children select play-mates of the same age. Developmentally delayed children may choose to play with younger children because their developmental level is more similar. Children with poor social skills may also play with younger children. It is important to assess the availability of peer-age friends, the child's developmental level and the previous relationship between the children to determine if sexual behaviors between children of different ages are problematic. In general, the wider the age difference, the greater the concern.

3. Sexual behaviors are out of balance with other aspects of the child's life and interests. Children are interested in every aspect of their environment from the sun rising to how babies are made. While children may explore some aspects of their world more extensively at certain periods of their young lives, their interests are generally broad and intermittent. Children's sexual behavior follows the same pattern. At one period they may be very interested in learning about sexuality and another time about how the dishwasher works or what will make Mommy and Daddy mad. Many fluctuations occur in a day, a week and a month. When a child is preoccupied with sexuality, this raises concern. If a child would prefer to masturbate rather than engage in regular childhood activities, this raises concern.

4. Children who seem to have too much knowledge about sexuality and behave in ways more consistent with adult sexual expression. As children develop, they acquire knowledge about sex and sexuality from television, movies, videos, magazines, their parents, relatives, school and other children. This knowledge is generally assimilated, without disruption, into the child's developing understanding of sex and sexuality; this translates into additional natural and healthy sexual interest. When children have been overexposed to explicit adult sexuality, pornography, environments with poor boundaries, or sexual abuse, they may engage in or talk about sexual behaviors that are beyond age-appropriate sexual knowledge and interest.

5. Sexual behaviors are significantly different than those of other same-age children. The frequency and type of children's sexual behaviors depend, to a certain extent, on the environment (home, neighborhood, culture, religion) in which they have been raised, their parents' and siblings' attitudes and actions related to sex and sexuality, and their peers' behaviors. If a child's sexual behavior stands out among his or her peers, this raises concern. Teachers from schools that serve neighborhood populations are very good resources to consult in evaluating whether a child's sexual behaviors are similar to his or her peers.

6. Sexual behaviors continue in spite of consistent and clear requests to stop. While adults may be inconsistent regarding other behaviors and children may persist in engaging in them, children generally learn very quickly that there is a strong taboo on openly engaging in sexual behavior. While most adults are consistent about telling children to stop sexual behaviors, some are not. Inconsistent messages regarding sexual behavior may sustain or increase a child's sexual behaviors.

Children's sexual behaviors that continue in the view of adults, despite consistent requests to stop or even punishment, may be a conscious or unconscious method of indicating that they need help. When children "cry for help" they may persist in the behavior until adults pay heed, discover, and/or change the causes of the sexual behavior.

Some children have learned to dissociate during times of stress. While they are "spaced out" they may engage in sexual behavior that is an attempt to decrease their anxiety. If this is happening, the child may be unaware of what he or she is doing. Because the child's response to stress is to "space out" and engage in sexual behaviors, it may happen in spite of consistent requests to stop.

7. Children appear unable to stop themselves from engaging in sexual activities. Some children appear to feel driven to engage in sexual behaviors, even though they will be punished or admonished. Generally, this type of sexual behavior is in response to things that go on around them or feelings which reawaken memories that are traumatic, painful, overly stimulating or of which they can't make sense. The child may respond by masturbating or engaging in other sexual behaviors alone or with children or adults. Hiding the sexual behaviors or finding friends to engage in the behaviors in private may not be possible for these children. Sexual behavior that is driven by anxiety, guilt or fear often does not respond to normal limit setting. The sexual behavior is a way of coping with overwhelming feelings. This type of sexual behavior may not be within the full conscious control of the child.

While not yet known, it may be that some children who engage in more compulsive sexual behaviors have an excess of sex hormones, stress-related neurobiological or neurochemical changes in their brains, or physiological differences which drive this behavior.

8. Children's sexual behaviors elicit complaints from other children and/or adversely affect other children.

Generally, children complain when something is annoying or discomforting to them. When a young child complains about another child's sexual behaviors, it is an indication that the behavior is upsetting to the child and should be taken seriously. In natural and healthy sexual play both children agree, directly or indirectly, not to tell and engage in it willingly. It is quite unlikely that either would tell on the other; therefore, if one child is telling, this is a cause for concern.

Alternatively, on elementary school playgrounds, boys and girls run after one another discovering who has the most "cooties." When the children are equal in age, developmental status and are having fun together, these complaints are generally a spirited age-appropriate interchange that need only be monitored to see that it remains fun and non-coercive.

9. Children's sexual behaviors are directed at adults who feel uncomfortable receiving them. Children hug adults and give them kisses. These are generally spontaneous reflections of caring or because they have been told to kiss the adult (usually a relative) by a parent. When a child continues to touch an adult in a manner more like adult-adult sexual contact, offer themselves as sexual objects, or solicit sexual touch from adults, this raises concern.

10. Children (4 years and older) do not understand their rights or the rights of others in relation to sexual contact. Most parents teach their children by their own behavior about emotional, physical and sexual privacy. Generally, school-age children have developed an awareness of their own and others' personal space. If children are brought up in homes where their personal boundaries are violated, such as in emotional, sexual and/or physical abuse or intrusiveness, they may not learn the unwritten rules regarding personal space.

11. Sexual behaviors progress in frequency, intensity or intrusiveness over time. While sexual behavior in children is natural and healthy, the frequency is generally moderate, sporadic, and generally occurs outside the vision and knowledge of others. Since by elementary school, children increasingly hide their sexual behaviors from adults, if a child's sexual behaviors invade others' emotional and physical space, are increasing, and are known to adults, this raises concern.

12. Fear, anxiety, deep shame or intense guilt is associated with the sexual behaviors. Children's feelings regarding sexuality are generally light-hearted, spontaneous, giggly or silly. In some cases, if a child has been caught engaging in sexual behaviors, the adult's response may generate embarrassed or guilty feelings in the child. Yet, these feelings are qualitatively different than the deep shame, intense guilt, fear or anxiety of a child who has been fooled, coerced, bribed or threatened into sexual behaviors or overexposed to adult sexuality, particularly sexuality paired with aggressive feelings or actions.

13. Children engage in extensive, persistent mutually agreed upon adult-type sexual behaviors with other children.

Children generally engage in a variety of spontaneous and sporadic sexual behaviors with other children for purposes of exploration and the satisfaction of curiosity. Some children who feel alone in the world may turn to other children to decrease their loneliness. These children often do not see adults as sources of emotional warmth and caring. If the children have been prematurely sexualized and/or taught that sex equals caring, they may try to use sex as a way to cope with their loneliness and feelings of abandonment (See top of page 24).

14. Children manually stimulate or have oral or genital contact with animal/s. Children in urban and suburban areas rarely have contact with the genitalia of animals. Children on farms might have some sexual contact with animals but it is limited. Children who engage in repeated sexualized behaviors with animals or who harm animals raise concern.

15. Children sexualize nonsexual things, interactions with others, or relationships. For example, the child imagines "she wants to be my girlfriend," or "he is thinking about doing sex" without any observable basis for thinking this. When a child, more often than his or her peers, sees everyday objects as sexual, or sees people as only sexual objects, this is a concern.

16. Sexual behaviors cause physical or emotional pain or discomfort to self or others. When a child's interest in things related to sex and sexuality intrudes on others' emotional or physical privacy or body space making them uncomfortable, this is cause for concern. If the child's sexual behaviors are causing them or others physical pain, this creates additional concern.

17. Children use sex to hurt others. When sex and pain, sex and disappointment, sex and hurt, sex and jealousy or sex and other negative emotions and experiences have been paired in the child's home environment, the child may learn to use sex as a weapon. Angry sexual language and gestures, as well as sexual touching, become a way to get back at people. In domestic violence this pairing of sex with negative emotions and harm almost always occurs.

18. Verbal and/or physical expressions of anger precede, follow or accompany the sexual behavior. In healthy development, sexual expression and exploration is accompanied by positive emotions. Verbal or physical aggression that accompanies children's sexual behaviors or language is a learned response. In general, children who repeat this behavior have witnessed repeated instances of verbally and/or physically aggressive behavior that has occurred in the context of their caregivers' relationships. While continuous viewing of sex and aggression on the television, in films and videos can have very negative effects on young children, experiences in their homes are far more damaging. When children see or hear their parents or caregivers using sexual language or gestures in aggressive ways, they learn from it.

When children use bad language it is generally with each other and out of the earshot of adults. If young children are using sexual language in a violent way and directing it at others, this is cause for concern.

19. Children use distorted logic to justify their sexual actions. ("She didn't say no.") When caught doing something wrong, children often try to make an excuse to avoid blame and responsibility. It is valuable to see if their rationalizations, denial and justifications are similar across all negative behaviors or specific to the sexual behaviors. When young children make excuses about their sexual behaviors that disregard others' rights or deny responsibility for troublesome sexual behaviors, this raises concern.

20. Coercion, force, bribery, manipulation or threats are associated with sexual behaviors. Healthy sexual exploration may include some teasing or daring; unhealthy sexual expression involves the use of emotional or physical force or coercion to engage another child in sexual behavior. Children who engage in coercive sexual behavior may find a child who is emotionally or physically vulnerable to coerce into the sexual behavior. Although infrequent in young children, groups of children may use sex to hurt other children.

CHARTS ON BEHAVIORS RELATED TO SEX AND SEXUALITY IN YOUNG CHILDREN

The following charts use sexual behaviors of children with normal intelligence to illustrate how a particular sexual behavior may be natural and healthy unto itself, but when it is characterized by one or more of the 20 characteristics described previously, it becomes problematic. Where the behavior takes place, how the behavior is discovered and the relationship between the persons involved are important in assessing its seriousness.

These charts are a step in defining behaviors related to sex and sexuality that are natural and healthy, behaviors that raise concern, and behaviors that require immediate consultation. Research by Friedrich (1998) asked mothers about sexual behaviors they observed their children engaging in. While not considering as many sexual behaviors, nor for the same purpose, with very few exceptions his research provides strong support for these charts.

The charts are *not* meant for use in determining if a child has been sexually abused. Children engaged in any behavior in any column may or may not have been sexually abused. Johnson (1995) describes how to assess the sexual behaviors of a child when investigating allegations of child sexual abuse.

The behaviors in the *first column* are those that are in the expected range. This range is wide; some children may engage in several of the behaviors while some may engage in none. If a child engages in most or all of the behaviors, this raises concern.

The *second column* describes behaviors that are seen in children who are overly concerned about sex and sexuality for their age and developmental level. When a child shows several of these behaviors, or the behavior persists in spite of interventions, consultation with a professional is advised.

The *third column* describes behaviors that are often indicative of a child who is experiencing deep confusion in the area of sexuality. This child may or may not have experienced hands-on abuse of some kind. It may be that the level of sexual confusion and/or aggression in the environment in which the child has lived overwhelmed the child's ability to integrate it, and the child is acting out the confusion. Consultation with a qualified professional who specializes in child sexuality or child abuse should be sought.

BEHAVIORS RELATED TO SEX AND SEXUALITY IN PRESCHOOL CHILDREN

Natural and Healthy	Of Concern	Seek Professional Help
Touches/rubs own genitals when diapers are being changed, when going to sleep, when tense, excited or afraid.	Continues to touch/rub genitals in public after being told consistently not to do this.	Touches/rubs self to the exclusion of normal childhood activities. Hurts own genitals by touching/rubbing.
Explores differences between males and females, boys and girls.	Asks continuous questions about genital differences after all questions have been answered.	Plays male or female roles in an angry, sad or aggressive manner. Hates own/other sex.
Touches the "private parts" of familiar adults and children.	Touches the "private parts" of adults not in family, or unknown children, or familiar people after being told "no." Asks to be touched him/herself.	Sneakily touches adults. Makes others allow his/her touching, demands that others touch him/her.
Takes advantage of opportunity to look at nude people.	Stares at nude people even after having seen many people nude.	Asks people to take off their clothes. Tries to forcibly undress people.
Asks about the genitals, breasts, intercourse, babies.	Keeps asking people even after parent has answered all questions at an age appropriate level.	Asks unfamiliar people after parent has answered all questions. Sexual knowledge too great for age.
Erections	Continuous erections	Painful erections
Likes to be nude. May show others his/her genitals.	Wants to be nude in public after the parent repeatedly and consistently says "no."	Refuses to put on clothes. Secretly shows "private parts" in public after many scoldings.
Interested in watching people doing bathroom functions.	Interest in watching bathroom functions does not wane after days/weeks.	Refuses to leave people alone in bathroom. Forces way into bathroom.

BEHAVIORS RELATED TO SEX AND SEXUALITY IN PRESCHOOL CHILDREN

Natural and Healthy	Of Concern	Seek Professional Help
Interested in having/ birthing a baby.	Boys' interest does not wane after several days/ weeks of play about babies.	Displays fear or anger about babies, birthing or intercourse.
Uses "dirty" words for bathroom and sexual functions.	Continues to use "dirty" words at home after parent consistently says "no," and parents do not swear.	Uses "dirty" words in public and at home after many strong scoldings and parents do not swear.
Interested in own feces.	Smears feces on walls or floor more than one time.	Repeatedly plays or smears feces after scolding.
Plays "doctor" inspecting others' bodies, including "private parts."	Frequently plays "doctor" and gets caught, after being consistently told not to play it.	Forces child to take off clothes and play "doctor."
Puts something in own genitals or rectum one time *for curiosity or exploration.*	Puts something in genitals or rectum of self or other after being told "no."	Any coercion, force, pain in putting something in genitals or rectum of self or other child.
Plays house, acts out roles of Mommy and Daddy.	Humping other children with clothes on after being told not to.	Simulated or real intercourse without clothes, oral genital contact.

BEHAVIORS RELATED TO SEX AND SEXUALITY IN KINDERGARTEN THROUGH FOURTH GRADE CHILDREN

Natural and Healthy	Of Concern	Seek Professional Help
Asks about the genitals, breasts, intercourse, babies.	Shows fear or anxiety about sexual topics.	Asks endless questions about sex after curiosity satisfied. Sexual knowledge too great for age.
Interested in watching/ peeking at people doing bathroom functions.	Keeps getting caught watching/peeking at others doing bathroom functions.	Refuses to leave people alone in bathroom.
Uses "dirty" words for bathroom functions, genitals, and sex.	Uses "dirty" words with adults after parent consistently says "no," punishes child, and uses healthy language themselves.	Continues use of "dirty" words even after exclusion from school and activities.
Plays "doctor," inspecting others' bodies, including "private parts."	Frequently plays "doctor" and gets caught after being told "no."	Forces child to take clothes off and play doctor.
Boys and girls are interested in having/ birthing a baby.	Boy keeps making believe he is having a baby after month/s.	Child displays fear or anger about babies or intercourse.
Shows others his/her genitals in a private location.	Shows genitals in public after the parent says "no" and punishes child.	Shows genitals at school and/or other places to express anger.
Interest in urination and defecation.	Plays with feces. Purposely urinates outside of toilet bowl.	Repeatedly plays with or smears feces. Purposely urinates on furniture, etc.
Touches/rubs own genitals when going to sleep, when tense, excited or afraid.	Continues to touch/ rub genitals in public after being told "no" consistently. Rubs genitals on furniture or other objects.	Touches/rubs self in public or in private to the exclusion of normal childhood activities. Rubs genitals on people.

BEHAVIORS RELATED TO SEX AND SEXUALITY IN KINDERGARTEN THROUGH FOURTH GRADE CHILDREN

Natural and Healthy	Of Concern	Seek Professional Help
Plays house, may simulate all roles of Mommy and Daddy.	Repeatedly humping other children with clothes on. Repeatedly imitates sexual behavior with dolls/stuffed toy.	Humping naked. Intercourse with another child. Forcing sexual contact on a child or adult.
Thinks other gender children are "gross" or have "cooties." Chases them.	Uses "dirty" language after other children *really* complain.	Uses bad language against other child's family. Hurts other gender children.
Talks about sex with friends. Talks about having a girl/boy friend.	Sex talk gets child in trouble. Romanticizes all relationships.	Talks about sex and sexual acts habitually. Repeatedly in trouble with regard to sexual talk.
Wants privacy when in bathroom or changing clothes.	Becomes very upset when observed changing clothes.	Aggressive or fearful in demand for privacy.
Likes to hear and tell "dirty" jokes, makes a few sexual sounds.	Keeps getting caught telling "dirty" jokes or making sexual sounds, e.g. sighs, moans.	Still gets caught telling "dirty" jokes, or making sexual sounds, even after exclusion from school and fun activities.
Plays games with same-aged children related to sex and sexuality.	Wants to play games with much younger/ older children related to sex and sexuality.	Child or children force others to play sexual games that make them uncomfortable.

BEHAVIORS RELATED TO SEX AND SEXUALITY IN KINDERGARTEN THROUGH FOURTH GRADE CHILDREN

Natural and Healthy	Of Concern	Seek Professional Help
Draws genitals on human figures for artistic expression or because figure is being portrayed in the nude.	Draws genitals on some nude figures but not others or on drawings of clothed people. Genitals disproportionate to size of body.	Genitals stand out as most prominent feature of drawing. Drawings of intercourse, group sex, sex with animals, sadism, or masochism.
Explores differences between adult males and females, boys and girls.	Confused about male/female differences after all questions have been answered.	Plays male or female roles in a sad, angry or aggressive manner. Hates own/other gender.
Takes advantage of opportunity to look at nude people.	Stares/sneaks to stare at nude people after punishment and having seen many people nude.	Asks others to take off their clothes. Tries to forcibly undress children or adults.
Pretends to be opposite gender.	Talks very negatively about own gender.	Hates/fears being own gender. Hates own genitals.
Wants to compare genitals with peer-aged friends.	Wants to compare genitals with much older or much younger people.	Demands to see the genitals, breasts, or buttocks of others.
Looks at the genitals, buttocks, or breasts of others.	Stares at the genitals, breasts, or buttocks of others making them uncomfortable.	Continuously sneaks and peeks at genitals, breasts, or buttocks of others after being caught many times.
Interest in touching genitals, breasts, or buttocks of other same-age child or have child touch his/hers.	Makes others uncomfortable by requests to touch their genitals, breasts, or buttocks or have them touch his/her genitals, breasts, or buttocks.	Coerces unwilling child to touch his or her genitals, breasts, or buttocks or allow touching of theirs. Forced or mutual oral, anal, or vaginal sex.

BEHAVIORS RELATED TO SEX AND SEXUALITY IN KINDERGARTEN THROUGH FOURTH GRADE CHILDREN

Natural and Healthy	Of Concern	Seek Professional Help
Kisses familiar adults and children. Allows kisses by familiar adults and children.	French kissing. Talks in sexualized manner with others. Fearful of hugs and kisses by adults. Gets very anxious when sees displays of affection. Kisses unfamiliar adult or child.	Talks/acts in a sexualized manner with unknown adults. Physical contact with any adult causes agitation, fear or anxiety to the child or adult.
Looks at nude pictures.	Continuous fascination with nude pictures that gets child in trouble.	Wants to masturbate to nude pictures or display them.
Erections	Continuous erections or fear of erection.	Painful erections or hurting self to stop erection.
Puts something in own genitals/rectum for the physical sensation, curiosity or exploration.	Puts something in own genitals/rectum frequently or when it feels uncomfortable. Puts something in the genitals/rectum of other child.	Any coercion or force in putting something in genitals/rectum of other child. Causing harm to own/others genitals/ rectum.
Interest in breeding behavior of animals.	Touching genitals of animals.	Sexual behaviors with animals.

HAS MY CHILD BEEN SEXUALLY ABUSED?

In the 1980's and 1990's it was believed that if a child engaged in problematic sexual behaviors it was due to having been sexually abused (Friedrich, 1997; Friedrich et al., 1992; Slusser, 1995). After substantial study, we now know that this is generally not the case. Some children who engage in the behaviors listed in the last two columns on the charts have been sexually abused but *most* have not been sexually abused (Drach, Wientzen et al., 2001; Friedrich, 2002; Silovsky & Niec, 2002). There are many things that influence the development of problematic sexual behaviors (See page 3-5), and actual hands-on sexual abuse is only one of the many. If you are concerned about your child's sexual behaviors, consult a qualified mental health professional with expertise in child abuse or call child protective services (CPS) (See below).

DO VICTIMS OF SEXUAL ABUSE BECOME PERPETRATORS OF SEXUAL ABUSE?

The media encourages the popular belief of an almost inevitable leap from childhood sexual abuse to sexual offending. This is *not* supported by research. While there is an increased risk of later delinquent and adult criminal activity <u>for all maltreated children,</u> most child sexual abuse victims do not go on to become offenders of any kind (Widom, 1994). Research on the impact of abuse finds substantial groups of victims who appear to have little symptomatology (Kendall-Tackett, Williams, & Finkelhor, 1993; Sirles, Smith, & Kusama, 1989; Gratz & Orsillo, 2003). Sexually abused children are found to have less symptomatology than other children in outpatient mental health clinics (Friedrich, 2002; Young, 1992). Factors that may decrease the negative effects of sexual abuse are characteristics of the abusive incident (less severe), child characteristics (good coping skills) or the child's environment (a relationship with a significant and supportive person) (Widom, 1994).

Research also points out that most adult and adolescent perpetrators of sexual abuse were *not* sexually victimized as children. According to Hanson and Slater's (1988) review of numerous samples, 20-30% of adult sex offenders were child sexual abuse victims. Ryan, Miyoshi et al. (1996), in a review of 90 programs specifically designed to treat adolescents who sexually offend, found that 40% of the 1,600 adolescents had been sexually abused and 40% had been physically abused.

Parents worry that if their child has been sexually abused, he or she will go on to sexually molest other children. In a sample of 339 child welfare and mental health professionals, 21% said they had been sexually abused when they were 12 or younger. Of the people who said they were sexually abused, 97% answered "no" to the question, "When you were twelve or younger, did you coerce a child twelve or younger into any behaviors related to sex and sexuality?" (Johnson & Mitra, 2007) Drach (Drach, Wientzen, & Ricci, 2001) studied a group of children from a forensic child abuse clinic and found no significant relationship between being a victim of sexual abuse and the presence or absence of sexual behavior problems. Children who have been sexually abused are unjustifiably seen as at substantial risk to molest (Friedrich & Chaffin, 2000).

Parents who think sexual victims become perpetrators sometimes act differently toward their child. This can include not touching, hugging, cuddling, wrestling or kissing the child; watching all of the child's actions expecting negative behaviors; and looking for disturbed sexual behaviors. This can be very detrimental to a child's sense of self and can increase the child's feelings of being "bad" or "damaged goods" after abuse. There is no published literature on child sexual abuse victims becoming sexual offenders at any time in their lives when they are treated respectfully, believed, provided therapeutic support when needed, protected from further abuse, and when their family (or substitute family) provides them with a nurturing and healthy environment.

A CONTINUUM OF SEXUAL BEHAVIORS: FROM NATURAL AND HEALTHY TO CHILDREN WHO MOLEST

In the 1980s and early 1990s people thought that when children had sexual problems these problems were similar to those of adults. Studying children's sexual behavior problems has led to a clearer understanding. We now know that there are children with varying levels of sexual problems and that even when children do engage in sexual offending, it is very different from adult sexual offending.

There is a continuum of sexual behaviors in children, from natural and healthy to children who molest other children. The vast majority of children's sexual behavior is natural and healthy (See pages 1-2), yet there are some young children with sexual behavior problems. Children who have sexual behavior problems can be divided into three groups: (a) sexually-reactive, (b) children who engage in extensive, mutual sexual behaviors, and (c) children who molest other children.

The problematic sexual behaviors of "**sexually-reactive**" children are often done in view of adults and may be frequent. While these children can generally be distracted from engaging in the behaviors, they often erupt again. Many of the behaviors are self-directed or may be directed toward others, including adults. If these children engage in sexual behaviors with other children, there is no coercion or force used, although receiving sexual behaviors can be confusing and feel like a violation or abuse. If a child says "no" the sexually-reactive child simply finds another child. The other person is often incidental as the sexual behaviors are not directed at them in anger or for retaliation. Confusion, fear, and anxiety about sex, which is driven by the child's history, is fundamental to this type of sexual behavior. The sexually-reactive behaviors are a way of trying to understand or work through this confusion and to reduce their anxiety. Frequently, there are readily identifiable triggers in the immediate environment of the child or in the child's thoughts and feelings that precede the sexual behavior. Some of these children have been sexually abused in a hands-on way, others have not (See pages 3-5). Some of these children report sexual arousal while most do not. This is by far the largest of the three groups of children with sexual behavior problems.

The sexual behaviors of "**children who engage in extensive mutual sexual behavior**" are frequent, often habitual and may include the full spectrum of adult sexual behaviors. Often distrustful, chronically hurt and abandoned by adults, these children relate best to other children. In the absence of close, supportive relationships to adults, the sexual behaviors are a way of coping with feelings of abandonment, loss and fear. While these children do not generally have close emotional relationships with the other child or children with whom they engage in the sexual behaviors, they do feel a "connection" which decreases their sense of isolation and lack of attachments to adults. The sexual

behavior is generally difficult to stop, as the children do not see it as "wrong," but as a way of feeling emotionally safer. They may use persuasion, but there is no coercion. They find willing partners who also feel "lost" who will collude with them to avoid detection by their parents/caretakers. Some of these children report sexual arousal while most do not. This is the second largest group of children with sexual behavior problems, but much smaller than the sexually-reactive group.

The sexual behaviors of "**children who molest**" are frequent and pervasive. A growing pattern of sexual behavior problems is evident in their histories. Intense sexual confusion is a hallmark of their thinking and behavior. Sexuality and aggression are closely linked in the thoughts and actions of these children. Unless the other child is too young to understand, children who molest use some type of coercion to gain participation in the sexual behaviors. Bribery, trickery, manipulation or emotional or physical coercion are generally used. Physical force is not commonplace, nor necessary, as the children's victims are selected due to special vulnerabilities, including developmental delays, social isolation and emotional neediness. The victims may be older, younger or the same age. There is an impulsive and aggressive quality to many of the behaviors of these children, including their sexual behaviors. These children generally have problems in all areas of their lives. Some of these children report sexual arousal while most do not. There are very few children who sexually offend, but when identified, they need very specialized help.

IS THERE HELP FOR CHILDREN WITH SEXUAL BEHAVIOR PROBLEMS?

"Sexually-reactive" children, "children with extensive mutual sexual behaviors" and "children who molest" can all be helped to stop the problematic sexual behaviors. Children engaging in problematic sexual behaviors have observed too much adult sexuality, lived in environments that have confused them, and some have been sexually abused in a "hands-on" manner. Children are like sponges that absorb the behaviors, values, attitudes and feelings of those around them. These children have learned behaviors, attitudes and feelings that can be unlearned. It is important to remember that the worrisome sexual behaviors are just developing; there are no deeply rooted patterns to the sexual behaviors. Children change rapidly as they grow up. They are very malleable and can absorb healthy attitudes, behaviors and feelings about sex and sexuality. Providing a sexually healthy and safe environment for children with sexual behavior problems is essential for their future development.

It is important not to confuse children with sexual behavior problems with adults with sexual behavior problems. Unfortunately, this confusion is still common and has led to the belief that these children will continue to have sexual problems all of their lives. There is no clinical support for this belief. In fact, with a thorough assessment to understand the cause for the problematic sexual behaviors and cognitive behavior therapy, most children with sexual behavior problems can be helped in a few months (Johnson, 2002; Bonner, Walker, & Berliner, 1999; Carpentier, Silovsky, & Chaffin, 2006).

The belief that "children who molest" are just small versions of adult sexual offenders has led to children (12 and younger) being registered as sexual offenders *for life* in some states in the United States. Adult offenders' sexual problems are often rooted in deeply ingrained patterns of deviant sexual arousal and response. This is not true of children who generally are not experiencing sexual arousal and do not have identifiable sexual arousal patterns. To condemn a child to a life long label as a sexual offender when there is no evidence that this will be true is unjustified. Most adults would not want to be labeled for life for their childhood misbehaviors, no matter how serious. In an anonymous survey of 339 child welfare and mental health professionals, 4.5% said they coerced another child into sexual behaviors when they were 12 and younger (Johnson & Mitra, 2007).

GETTING HELP

After reading the above material you may have decided your child's sexual behaviors are natural and healthy. However, if you are worried, you can call a qualified mental health professional familiar with child sexuality or child abuse and ask for an evaluation. Community mental health centers, university counseling centers, pediatricians, and hospitals may have referrals. If you think there may be a medical problem, call your pediatrician. You can also call Child Protective Services (CPS) or the police for referrals.

CALLING CHILD PROTECTIVE SERVICES (CPS) AND/OR THE POLICE

In the United States all people who work with children are legally mandated reporters of *suspected* abuse. This means that CPS or the police *must* be notified (call the Child Abuse Hotline or ask the Operator for assistance) if the mandated reporter suspects abuse whether by a child, adolescent, or adult. Anyone, regardless of his or her relationship to a child, who suspects child abuse *can* call to file a concern.

Sexual behaviors of children that are outside what is considered natural and healthy *may* be an indication of some type of abuse or neglect to them or someone close to them. If a child's sexual behaviors are characterized by several of the 20 characteristics, or the child is engaging in several of the behaviors in Columns 2 and/or 3 on the charts, and there is no healthy explanation, the child will benefit from a professional evaluation. If you are not sure, you can call CPS and discuss whether the behaviors you are seeing require professional assessment.

Gather as much pertinent data as possible before phoning. Collect information such as: the child's behavior at home and school; the type, frequency and characteristics of any problematic sexual behavior; and any other information which indicates the child or family is experiencing difficulty. CPS needs solid information to decide how to respond to calls.

CPS does not disclose the name of the person who files a suspected child abuse report.

REFERENCES

Bonner, B., Walker, C. E., & Berliner, L. (1999). Children with sexual behavior problems: Assessment and treatment. *http://www.childwelfare.gov/search/view_pubs.cfm?pubs_search=1&keyword1=children+with+sexual+behavior+problems.*

Carpentier, M., Silovsky, J., & Chaffin, M. (2006). Randomized trial of treatment for children with sexual behavior problems: ten-year follow-up. *Journal of Consulting and Clinical Psychology,* 74(3), 482-488.

Connolly, M. (2001). *Developmental trajectories: Sexual aggression and childhood sexuality.* Doctoral dissertation, University of Canterbury, New Zealand.

Drach, K., Wientzen, et al. (2001). The diagnostic utility of sexual behavior problems in diagnosing sexual abuse in a forensic child abuse evaluation clinic. *Child Abuse & Neglect, 25,* 489-503.

Finkelhor, D. (1983). *Childhood sexual experiences: A retrospective survey.* Unpublished manuscript, University of New Hampshire.

Friedrich, W. (1991). Sexual behavior in sexually abused children. In J. Briere (Ed.), *Treating Victims of Child Sexual Abuse* (pp.15-27). New York: Jossey-Bass, Inc.

Friedrich, W. (2002). Child sexual behavior inventory: Normative, psychiatric and sexual abuse comparisons. *Child Maltreatment, 6*(1), 37-49.

Friedrich, W., & Chaffin, M. (2000). *Developmental-systemic perspectives on children with sexual behavior problems.* San Diego, CA: Association for the Treatment of Sexual Abusers.

Friedrich, W. N., Davies, W., Feher, E., & Wright, J. (2003). Sexual behavior problems in preteen children: Developmental, ecological, and behavioral correlates. *Annals of the New York Academy of Sciences, 989,* 95-104.

Friedrich, W., Fisher, J., Broughton, D., Houston, M., & Shafran, C. (1998). Normative sexual behavior in children: A contemporary sample. *Pediatrics, 101* (4).

Friedrich, W., Grambsch, P., Damon, L., Koverola, C., Hewitt, S., Lang, R., & Wolfe, V. (1992). The child sexual behavior inventory: Normative and clinical comparisons. *Psychological Assessment, 4*(3), 303-311.

Friedrich, W. (1997). *Child sexual behavior inventory professional manual.* Odessa, FL: Psychological Assessment Resources, Inc.

Gratz, K. L., & Orsillo, S. M. (2003). Scientific expert testimony in child sexual abuse cases: Legal, ethical, and scientific considerations. Clinical Psychology: Research and Practice, 10, 358-363.

Gil, E., & Johnson, T. C. (1993). *Sexualized children: Assessment and treatment of sexualized children and children who molest.* Rockville, MD: Launch Press.

Goldman, R., & Goldman, J. (1988). *Show me yours - Understanding children's sexuality.* Penguin Books.

Hanson, R., & Slater, S. (1988). Sexual victimization in the history of sexual abusers: A review. *Annals of Sex Research, 1*, 485-499.

Haugaard, J., & Tilly, C. (1988). Characteristics predicting children's responses to sexual encounters with other children. *Child Abuse and Neglect, 12*, 209-218.

Johnson, T. C. (1988). Child perpetrators - children who molest other children: Preliminary findings. *Child Abuse and Neglect, 12*, 219-229.

Johnson, T. C. (1991). Understanding the sexual behaviors of children, *SIECUS Report*, August/September.

Johnson, T. C. (1995). Assessing young children's sexual behaviors in the context of child sexual abuse evaluations. In T. Ney (Ed.), *True and false allegation of child sexual abuse assessment and case management* (pp. 49-72). New York: Brunner/Mazel.

Johnson, T. C. (1998). Children who molest. In W. Marshall, S. Hudson, T. Ward, & Y. Fernandez (Eds.), *Sourcebook of treatment programs for sexual offenders.* New York: Plenum.

Johnson, T. C. (2002). Treatment exercises for abused children and children with sexual behavior problems. www.tcavjohn.com

Johnson, T. C. & Mitra, R. (2007). *A retrospective study of children's (twelve and younger) sexual behaviors.* Manuscript submitted for publication.

Kendall-Tackett, K. A., Williams, L., Finkelhor, D. (1993). Impact of sexual abuse on children: A review and synthesis of recent empirical studies. *Psychological Bulletin, 113* (1), 164-180.

Larsson, I., & Svedin, C.G. (2001, September). Sexual experiences in childhood - Young adults' recollections. *Archives of Sexual Behavior.*

Ryan, G., T., Miyoshi, et al. (1996). Trends in a national sample of sexually abusive youths. *Journal of the American Academy of Child and Adolescent Psychiatrists, 35*(1), 17-25.

Silovsky, J., & Niec, L. (2002). Characteristics of young children with sexual behavior problems: A pilot study. *Child Maltreatment, 7*(3).

Sirles, E., Smith, J., & Kusama, H. (1989). Psychiatric status of intrafamilial child sexual abuse victims. *Journal of the American Academy of Child & Adolescent Psychiatry, 28*, 225-229.

Slusser, M. (1995). Manifestations of sexual abuse in preschool-aged children. *Issues in Mental Health Nursing, 16*, 481-491.

Widom, C., & Ames, M. (1994). Criminal consequences of childhood sexual victimization. *Child Abuse & Neglect, 18*(4), 303-318.

Young, L. (1992). Sexual abuse and the problem of embodiment. *Child Abuse & Neglect, 16*, 89-100.